I0203655

FREE VERSE EDITIONS

Edited by Jon Thompson

THESE BEAUTIFUL LIMITS

THESE
BEAUTIFUL
LIMITS

Thomas David Lisk

Parlor Press
West Lafayette, Indiana
www.parlorpress.com

Parlor Press LLC, West Lafayette, Indiana 47906

© 2006 by Parlor Press
All rights reserved.

Printed in the United States of America
S A N: 2 5 4 - 8 8 7 9

Library of Congress Cataloging-in-Publication Data

Lisk, Thomas D. (Thomas David)
  These beautiful limits / Thomas David Lisk.
      p. cm. -- (Free verse editions)
  ISBN 1-932559-97-3 (hardcover : acid-free paper) -- ISBN 1-
932559-96-5 (pbk. : acid-free paper) -- ISBN 1-932559-98-1
(adobe ebook)
    I. Title.

PS3612.I85T47 2006
811'.6--dc22

 2006031315

Printed on acid-free paper.

Cover illustration: "Self-Improvement" by Anastasia Osolin. Used
    by permission.

Parlor Press, LLC is an independent publisher of scholarly and
trade titles in print and multimedia formats. This book is available in
print and Adobe eBook formats from Parlor Press on the Internet
at http://www.parlorpress.com. For submission information or to
find out about Parlor Press publications, write to Parlor Press, 816
Robinson St., West Lafayette, Indiana, 47906, or e-mail editor@
parlorpress.com.

CONTENTS

ACKNOWLEDGMENTS

I gratefully acknowledge the journals in which some of these poems appeared, sometimes in slightly different form:

Borderlands: "These Beautiful Limits"
Free Verse: "A Catalog of Ponies of the Pyrenees," "Shenango," and "Speech, Speech."
The Gut Cult: "Cheaper Mist," and "White Fixtures"

Thanks to my friends and (better) fellow poets for the role they played in shaping this collection: Alan Crist, Richard Getty, Mary Hennessy, Justin Marks, Aaron McCollough, Marjorie McNamara, Chris Salerno, and Chris Tonelli. Conversations with Steven B. Katz about poetry and publishing helped keep me going. Tim Botta has my deep appreciation for reading the whole manuscript carefully in its final stages and making useful suggestions. I owe special thanks to Jon Thompson for bravely taking a risk.

THESE BEAUTIFUL LIMITS

Double Cross

Burn this letter as soon as you have read it.
Feel free to take notes before you do.
As long as what you write is in your hand
and my name is nowhere affixed,
any connection will be conjectural,
entirely based on internal (and circumstantial) evidence.
In that sense nothing I have said is confidential,
though in the deepest possible sense
this message is meant for you alone
and therefore couldn't be more on guard for prying eyes.
How deep can a sense be? What's possible?
The wire hums hotly between us,
invigorating my heart with zaps,
but the lub dub continues as if nothing were wrong.
Plunge on as the sharp wire sings in.
Neutral third parties are the most dangerous.
They have a way of insinuating their own agendas.
And that's not just jargon. Let's sit on the veranda
and let candor inoculate us against specifics.
Such treatments are antique and volatile.
The wind bloweth where it listeth (modern: wishes)
Come all ye true-born tenement girls and listen unto me.
'Tis a tale of bitter perfidy, as you shall plainly see.
Ankles crossed under the table.

An Expedition

Walked out
the cat sough
Walked across
        prairie snout
Tread, we trod
        wanted a child's love
the me sum
        Clatsop basket
bliss of longing
        longing of desire
desire of body for body
        soul for body

Save Yourself

The border at which Alsace become Lorraine
and the leaf's edge and surfaces caress the air the leaf will someday join,
the full air reminding identity that what seems final,
the rearrangement of microscopic particles
to greet the eye in different forms,
the I dabbing its wet impressions
on the complex, infinitesimally moving surface
whose white sounds are so subtle
the softly bordered consciousness can hear them whispering and grinding
only as it slips momentarily across its own border
always dissolving into what it was not.
Meanwhile brush hairs find pockets to jab and fill with color
by unloading their own borders to enlarge the ones they meet.
This is as much as a consciousness can yield to the rest,
as much as the rest can prickle, can particle a mind.
Save yourself. Go ahead and try.

The Other Side, Sort Of

At last, the other side!
This world is just like that,
but empty of anxiety and longing.
Bicycle George wobbles a money wrench.
Working from memory swallows fly.
A map in red, white and blue might help.
Remember what it was I want to (blank).
Redoubtable winter follows spring at intervals.
Pictures of smiling youths are fly-blown and cracked.
A camera lies blind
in a black leather holster.
Arquebuses boom at kneeling Pequots.
The vizier orders the afreet back
into the ginger jar.
Each orange Japanese lantern
is lit by a red autumn seed.
From the western bank
a smiling boatman waves. Near the river
a black haired little girl folds origami lamps.
A scurrying brown insect suddenly takes to the air.
Lines from popular songs tie the captives' ankles.
Round patent leather toe caps turn into little ponds.
A dragonfly floats over tiny water.
Trees no bigger than almonds hide in the bushes.
Try to comprehend the night and its allergy to you.
Edna turns a steel key in a wine-red car.
Among the leaves random grey bugs roll in armored balls.
A former hero offers painted neckties to the street.
My head hurts and my neck is firm with tension.
A devotee of a pop sect swings a censer like a lantern.
A crowd gathers but no one drops change in the censer.
What the Abyssinian is continues what he was,
but empty of fear and desire.

A HORIZON

This mysterious simplicity comes of no conjuring but stands alone,
not displaying but not hiding the integrity of a quadratic house
with azure shutters and a glossy almost-azure door
through which wicked purveyors of iniquity (largely imaginary,
    or everyone) dare not pass,
and even good-hearted souls who offer free advice in black and
    white pamphlets
— advice in general enough terms so that it might apply to you —
cover their white shirts and bleached blouses before they rattle the
    door,
which, in the absence of a bell, is one way to try to get your
    attention.
The older one grows the more the mysterious entity processed as
    time seems to contain
(like an imaginary house) everything and nothing,
and all the secrets whose revelations now help us thrive are lined
    up horizontally beside us
because there is no vertical, and either the whole line marches
    together or nothing moves,
which is of course impossible, until one day you step ahead and
    disappear.
But the horizon remains, and the marchers, and memories of
    imaginary oblivion.

THE WORLD'S RELIGIONS

A dish of tea.
A complete thought.

A pure experience of space without time.
Usually not enough time.
Not to be spoken of limes.

Transmutation into unknow.
Tribes between Lascaux

and Sumeria, let's say people.
A precipice. Teeter.

A precise number of exact feathers arranged.
Aspiration. Aspirate H.

Opium, a white scent.
Mushroom chairs and legions of benches.

A locus, lice and locusts (not cicadas, science says).
Doxy and orthodoxy.

To be re. To be formed.
The present progressive without a subject.

Image and anti-image.
Profound puddle.

Sailing upon, on, in.
Let's be normal after all.

Air churning water, water churning dirt,
sand rushing palm bark.

Olive oil ceramic lamp. Whale fat.
Porcupine combs. Geezer.

Chrome sprocket, eye socket, orrery.
Odd vocabulary.

For one so young.
To one so old.

SIMPLE ENOUGH

He had a habit of.
What is a habit?
A candid blight of speculative soup,
a tic or a ticked list
against the ticking.
Let's say
a clock.

Loud sing cuckoo
fledged in a pre-owned
circle of twigs, leaves,
hair, string,
even a three-inch
strip of magenta ribbon.
Let's say purple.

A speckled egg.
How lovely, such form,
such delicacy of color.
Yet how easy!
Easier than the motley nest
wherein this elegant
and elemental,

this truth in bodily form
is laid and laid and laid.
The orioles return each
some season, and anyway,
the small birds,
the small birds make noises.
Let's say sing.

HAPPINESS RATIONING

Let's just do it. Sure it's cloudy,
but a light grey sky is perfect backdrop.
I never understood intaglio,
though I always liked the sound,
pronounce the tag or no.
The way the sound looks tickles me.
That smidge of creosote was once a neologism
in the feathery space between earth and Arthur.
When the minuscule driver is almost there,
he cringles the shiny dome bell
buckled to the crumpled handlebars
(peeling chrome fuzzy with rust)
and, glancing back at his load of passengers,
even though he hardly expected to see
the ones at the far rear, which must be near the equator,
says we're approaching our destination,
a whispery floating limit you can almost
see through the left-hand windows as we pass by.
I looked up from pictures of a famous singer
in the altogether I had folded—tucked, really, so they wouldn't
    get bent—
in my brass-cornered vinyl portfolio
just in time to catch a floating jingle,
but the darkened afterimage seemed to linger
on or in the window long enough so all I really heard
was a dog barking frantically,
and the screech of someone else's brakes.

CHEAPER MIST

This way is cheaper,
half the splintered conga,
minus the grommets,
no matter how tempted

you are by "however"—
Bastille Day in any other
month, and no excuses,
just the usual guarded

swerving against the light
on the right side
of a square curtain
threaded together

of bamboo thin
as tendrils escaping a coif.
You watch the untethered
kite with a wistful

feeling of farewell
as it wobbles and ducks
shallow in a sky
divided by swabs,

not sailors or short
Swabians but gobs of mist,
for a time
the most volatile of identities.

FORETASTE

The periodic table is a series of intervals
not a map stand. You may refer to it periodically
but it's not a periodical. Jumpy aren't you?

I forgot to mention a car door slammed
or a cat leaped on the sofa back, near your head.
Concentrate as best you can.

There are palliatives near the medicine chest.
Curved and shaking. Double Dover, up to fifty cents
a mile, discounting

gas wars foreclosed not triggered by oil wars,
a signal too. The unbearable levity of . . .

White Fixtures

Impulse hammer virtue into being.
All along the husk is cracking and a yellow tendril poking
toward the sun.

Keen! Alert!
The sound of toothed hammers everywhere.
Knives for handles.
Firm grip. Definite division.
Nubs and lumps.
No, and more no.

March, snake.
No pilfering grand dam here.

Another night has passed.
We have white fixtures.

Oh, great, more talkers!

THE SPANISH ARMADA

Right after a breakfast of spelt flour
bread on a plate and yerba maté in a mug reproducing
the third-class pottery
from The Lusitania, I got busy and surrounded
the Spanish Armada.
The enemy never had a chance against our superior
zeal and skill. The decks were red with gore.
Without our efforts
the Renaissance would have been a shower
of blood, all those illusions of bones built on bones, all that gilt, powder
and brocade smothered in rags stuffed in tortured prisoners'
mouths. But reason prevailed, persecution
diminished in key areas, after the predictable periods
of reactionary terror,
and possibilities began to pour
in all over the uninhabited shore.

Though rats were all too abundant on my fleet,
the good news was that the sea
breezes blew away all lighter-than-air creatures
smaller than seagulls, including anopheles,
carriers of fevers and disease,
so everyone who survived the fight was safe at least
temporarily, because, of course, by now we
knew none of the rats was rabid or carried
bubonic plague, for it's fleas not rats that are the real
culprits. And we know that now, thanks in some degree
to my single-minded efforts against those bloodthirsty Spaniards.

CONVERSING CONVERSELY

What is unreachable in us is the great mystery:
through us, by us, for us, with us,
after us, above us, around us.

The image condescends
to abstraction as if lousy with light,
the bubbling oatmeal face of small pox,

the polished blade in a story skirting violence.
You are what you can never become,
rowing slowly alone on a golden oval lake

skirted with gray-green trees,
a few signs, much paper on the forest floor,
aluminum, spit, feathers, leaves, needles.

Of like mind, we are.
The way you do I feel.
Think alike. We.

"These beautiful limits"

Emerson, "Experience"

Lafcadio became an adventurer.
Fate is kind.
Spoons nestle close but separate.
Wind carries rain.
Rain never carries wind.
Nothing in the engine is glass.
Mind is as elusive as soul.
Polly wolly doodle all the day.
The light among the leaves seems calm.
If there is ever a success you will not hear of it.
I can't run faster than the clock.
I can.
Nobody listens. Nobody.
What a thing to say.
Jimmy cracked corn and I don't care.
The cabin is empty.
A career is a duck blind.
Don't be shy about asking for lip gloss if the occasion demands it.
One day the dream gets up and walks away.
Falaral diddle all day.

FROM THE WIRE CIRCUSES

The air reeks of thick paper,
shelves crowded almost helter-skelter
with uprights and laterals,

motley and pleasing. Under soles,
yellow linoleum salted with gold
shifts to footsmooth

planks, the border a strip of grooved
aluminum. A rhomboid
you touch turns into a circus no bigger than a thick book.

Not a flea circus!

You can't say the elephants are miniature
unless you can determine
your own size. A gutter smells of nicotine

fingers.
The things
that interest
me are useless and never attract money.
A big plate window shimmering like mercury
looks out on colonial Ticonderoga.

SHENANGO

I have an urgent desire, almost a need, to write a novel called *Shenango*, a novel (from the Latin, *novus ordo seclorum*) in the sense of a book-length work of new imagination that would read like a fluent translation of a true story about the evening lands where emigrants go, seeking fulfillment but discovering a waste space where some have found fulfillment. Never be desperate. Let the darkest birds unfold their wings and clack their puppet beaks. Though their frightening unlikeness seems to require you to disintegrate, you must breathe back through your soft lips and nostrils as if in their minds you were incapable of either anger or depression, cloud-filled and blue-grounded as winter wildness from the height of a generously-peopled mountain where finally there is nothing for you to long for, only the pleasures of the other birds' aerial shenanigans.

With each iteration the cloud mass became spiffier, hollyhocks bloomed as delicate blue as hydrangeas and lilacs, only so subtly different from the explosion that is, or ought to be, pure white, drier and airier than powder, a limited number of monkeys in a tobacco box, the association being tales and iterations, charged by a beautiful armature of fine copper wires like incredibly attenuated claws, or better yet, cross-hatching on a drawing of the Gordian Knot (yes, there was only one). I say "claws" because jackdaws are all but (or anything but) unheard of here on Sullivan T. Coney's island, where the hares are gulls and take any pitch you toss them. The rest (a rest, rest) occurs across the wide Missouri. I long to see you. And what could seem emptier than air, more likely to arouse happy laughter than despair at your complete freedom of movement, except for the subtle pressures all around you, mounting as you mount higher, never looking up.

Now You See How We Live

The questions are not so difficult after all.
One by one they dissolve
like mother of pearl in magic water,
harmless to your fingers,

refreshing to your tongue.
Numbers and letters suddenly equal
other numbers and letters,
and joy blooms in a mood of great easing.

Tangled mysteries unknot,
braided hair shaken loose
from a ribbon that takes forever to float to the ground,
and you have forever to enjoy the fall.

The deepest secrets bob to the surface,
wink like amiable escorts on cool summer nights
and say, "Have your way with me."
Water at your feet is promising

to lap you into sleep.
New secrets are born hourly,
but they too evaporate in the dark,
though you might as well say "in the sun."

TALK ON THE CORNER

The sign says you will have afternoons to yourself next week,
but there's no telling how long the sign has been there, blandly
    asserting itself
like a silent fruit vendor too confident in the quality of his product
    to hawk
it with the vigor by which his competitors distinguish themselves.

"Talk on the corner," they call it, as if the weeds
in the cracks of the sidewalk were not concrete evidence that nature
    is reclaiming itself,
unaware that the difference between a weed and a wainscot
is value added—and, of course time to work time's bland deft

magic, as a thing that probably is not
shapes everything that is. And I use the word "thing" lightly,
figuring that it doesn't matter whether you characterize it
as animal, vegetable or mineral, it's the reason all of them are
    processes rather

than gold birds centered for the central emperor. Neither
the afternoons nor the emperor pays any attention to the sidewalk,
which is only part of the as yet indeterminate future,
like a Sunday morning that turns out to be a Wednesday

evening, evening outward to the timeless expanse
of all time, all day, every day.

THE SORORITY OF TIN-BEAKED VULTURES

When I think of telling you,
iron rises from the earth
and spatches the landscape
with orange squared girders.

When I think of telling you,
machinery cranks the carrousel
in spite of all the rust.

When I think of telling you,
nubbled fruit conceals
all it is perfectly willing to yield.

Far enough between poles,
tension seems so far it almost disappears.
A fluting voice for the cat
and bad jelly, misnamed of course,

blows through the polar air,
in name only,
a wandering emptiness
in which your stomach yields
to coriander and coffee-black soy
stirred by a loving hand,

and dark associations —
the sisterhood of raven hags,
the fraternal order of peppercorns and panthers,
the sorority of tin-beaked vultures —

spot the forest with their seed-healing shit.

Wittgensteiner Polka

Moore left the room and I don't believe it.
Not but.
This is a very good rojo but
why have they served me in a blanco glass?
Take out your doxology
and get down to the hard
business of utterly vapid.
Take the A cream.
The doctor asks me what's wrong.
I don't know, I tell her.
Something I'm breathing or feeling.
To treat you I need specifics.
I am specific, being specific.
It's not as if I don't have doubts.
Not to control other people, as with imprisonments and executions.
Arguing for love, which doesn't materialize.
As in a translation where you must look up even the most.
Youth didn't mind the outbuilding near the antique toward.
Technically correct.
No but.

THE FOWLER'S SNARE

The library is cold, but it makes sense,
it's cold outside. This is not air conditioning.
You've been in many hothouse libraries.
The cold is a relief at first.

I mean the cold outside. A chill, not refrigeration.
Fine knives rise from the earth's deep skin.
At first the cold is a relief.
The crisp corpus wants to dance among the volumes.

Ice seeps up from the frozen mantle.
The layer is warmed by neither sun nor magma.
The icy flesh and bones wants to jig among the books.
These are ideal working conditions.

The stratum of books is far between the sun and earth's hot core.
In the earth a bermed building seems safe.
Here between, the working conditions work.
Lake water lapping would be illusory.

Three to seven stories underground the wind never howls.
Without HVAC humming silence would be monumental.
The sound of lapping waves is only memory.
Down among the books, below the books, something —

Lacking fluorescent ballasts buzzing, the stillness would sing.
You've been in many an unbearably hot book room.
Down among the pages, under the spine, something waits.
The library is cold but is not heaven.

ELEPHANT SPOON

Wherever the weather wants to go. At least it keeps moving, almost always in a circular pattern. The talismanic moon in the neighborhood pulls neutrally. Anger encourages sensitivity to clouds one couldn't even see before. *Even*, the stump leg of moral relativity. Without it, the bond couldn't even totter. Tottering bond, unless you live in the tropics, I can't imagine why you would be interested in the nuances of tropical depression, but there it is, twenty-four hours per diem, the Weather Channel, endlessly reassuring information that actually is firm knowledge, just very temporary. Everything is moving, but but but *everything* creates a blur, and not just because it's moving. You didn't want to see pits in the razor's edge anyway. Nor do you want to think about all those steel blue and electroplated gold blades so beautifully and functionally designed and slipped used through a slot on the floor of the medicine chest to fall into the guts of a wall, an activity duplicated in so many homes for about a hundred years that someday creatures we can only imagine will wound their lips (they'll have to have lips) grazing where a surprise patch of razors has worked its way to the surface like a cache of fossilized sharks' teeth or flint flakes dropped by natives for thousands of years. And they will in their way know to be afraid of us. It rained yesterday. It rains again today.

Speech, Speech

To speak of fleeting Percivals
is never the work of a moment
but an undertaking
that must be undertaken
in due course and with a full sense
of the gravity of the occasion.
Nothing has,
and inevitably must again,
come of less.

The hall will, on that
august occasion, resound
anew with cheers to hearten
a heartless nation, now
bent upon a course that may
in the fullness of time
be vindicated, but which,
for now, must seem
to the thoughtful observer
self-destructive, to say the least.

An uncanny wind blows through
these affairs, riffling the numeral cards
on the far scoreboard, cards
lifted by a blunt hook
on a birchwood pole
some three
or four meters in length,
a pole
whose outer integument

might once have skinned
a lacustrine canoe.
Whose canoe, one is not
at liberty to divulge.

Thank you, thank you,
thank you, you have been,
as always, too
kind, too kind,
too kind.

A Catalog of Ponies
of the Pyrenees

1. Help! The seawall has caved.
2. One of the oceans threatens to engulf us.
3. The crowbar you sent was no use at all.
4. I would send it back but postage prohibits.

2. One of the oceans threatens to engulf us.
2. Sand can only do so much against water.
4. I would send it back but postal rules prohibit.
4. Send what back where?

1. Sand can only do so much.
1. Sand can't do anything; it's a victim.
3. Send what?
3. Imagine mailing a prybar packed in sand.

1. Sand is a victim.
2. I chased death all over the parking lot.
3. Imagine sending a sand-packed iron bar.
4. A well-placed blow crushed a grain to dust.

2. I chased death all over.
4. A blow from the bar broke the sand.
4. The soul would be a well-placed grain.
2. Aren't we all chasing death all the time?

4. The soul is the size of a transparent granule.
3. It has been customary to think of it as a thumb-sized flame.
2. Aren't we all hotly pursuing our ends?
1. A thumb would be a mighty large grain.

4. The soul is the size of a transparent granule.
2. Aren't we all hotly pursuing our ends?
2. Isn't each of us
4. the size of a granule?

3. The Upanishads mention a fat candle flame.
3. *Whose* custom depends on geography and language.
1. If it were flame-sized we could see it.
1. A flame under a collapsing seawall hasn't the ghost of a chance.

4. I wrapped it but the old frank marks took up too much space.
4. I had to use the paper over again, stamps and all.
2. Watching wind-driven water I can't identify the ocean.
2. If I didn't know better we could be on any coast.

4. After the floods subside, the crowbar will be useful.
3. Whose custom depends?
2. The threat is still imminent.
1. The seawall is down. Help!

OUTER

Gradually the tide of outer is moving this way,
the solitary sunflower blooming even in gray
rain it's somehow in collusion
with, flowering in its silver inwardness a compensation

for the brilliant brown and yellow everybody sees.
Sealed in arch speech of knowing — your knowing — the trees
and the river are safe from you who, like everyone,
know something that marks a big X over nothing,

that fluid, limpid network of rivers rippling over itself, reaching
to meet the tide lapping slowly up the disappearing beach,
the tan beach prickly with white lights bronze in the noon sun,
the particles of sun, coins with golden heads and silver tails,

golden blooms and slippery silver-filled stalks.
Rain and sun-bloom are mates, inmates of intimacy
Facing loneliness, conquering solitude seamlessly,
for all the outer is is walls of talk, walls of talk.

"DIVINE LIFE WARS UPON OUR OUTER LIFE."

Delft is blue as cobalt-glazed China.
People slide into marshes and inlets
where sweet eels catch bits of sky in their bare hands.
Women in starched white caps edged in eyelet lace
slither into you like tender eels
if you were not so limited to dreams in which
chronology makes perfect sense
and no one ever hits the pavement
or needs to rise and pee.
Who is who? you say.
I was wrong.
Vrou Vermeer caught the eels for dinner
on her way back to the surface (and eventually the sky)
through bottle green water weeds.

COMPANIONABLE SILENCE

A. VAGUE VACANCY

Incapable of gracious winnowing, loblolly succulence, the word
offers words, a helical nature.

I pasted your picture below—no, I glued it, cemented it.

Must I ask you to forgive me that I long for congress such as
crows must have or can't imagine?

Congress may be a mirror or the face in a mirror, either way
nothing you could call "real," bound up as it is with fleeting
singularities and ostrich feather ropes.

An ache to say something in a perfect circle with a center full
of an emptiness more precious and pure than "vacancy."

No vacancy.

Every nook properly crammed and the lobby teeming.

Frame sawn from loblolly and bullet-nailed rectangular and
plumb.

The vacancy of a motel attic.

How many times a day do you want to say, "That is the most
beautiful," easily fogging a darker knowledge of brutality,
superstitious fear and steel-clad certainties that evaporate
with the last breath.

One hopes uncertainties endure, a drive we take to endless
vacancies,

listening for emptiness to answer.

B. Void Answers

If I could but say the word I would become the answering
other.
"No" flooded with auxiliary lesser questions, a breeze lifts
while you're pumping gas.
What do you make of that?
Still, as it flows over you, you feel relieved, almost transported
free of time, the unimaginable.
But I keep telling you, you can escape time only by escaping
consciousness.
As if "now" meant anything to passages of air, which exists,
nameless, in eternity, the same way everything else does,
though eventually not as everything else.
Where would you run to anyway?
I wait for you everywhere and nowhere.
Your desire to annihilate each other diverts you momentarily.

C. Time

Today a goldfinch flies out of nowhere to an oak
from which a single yellow leaf floats down —
midsummer and all the clinging leaves are green.

ROBERT RAUSCHENBERG,
POSTER FOR PEACE, 1970

Traffic undulates under the Tappan Zee Bridge.
Black streets have the faintly salty taste
of sand whispering away gold.
All over the city railroad mattresses are smoldering.
Now and then a pillow bursts into flame.
Stockbrokers bid on catacombs while Mr. Ossuary Articulation sleeps
on the tar-spattered beach littered with condoms, syringes
and tampons like pink and white mice escaped from laboratory cages.
Herons mate with hermit crabs.
The pistol on the nightstand is highly polished licorice,
not soft and fresh, but still edible.
Should you poke the snub nose
between your gleaming teeth or toss
the unholstered weapon on your fresh-fluffed pillow?
Night falls, but it's only a wrinkled silk curtain,
the peculiar blue of one of the navies.

CHIN MUSIC

is not what you think,
not canzones or orange and iron ore emptiness
with a narrow line of foamy silver down deep in the distance
you would need a sure-footed saddle mule and a guide to reach;
not, chatter, but the natty curves and angles of young Gregory's
    fledgling beard,
orange and ochre and gold;
the runnels of Elnora's skin, dignified by dark rivers and soft light;
the yam-colored dribblings of baby (later great-grandma) Sadie's early
    lunches,
her first meals self-served with a padded apricot plastic spoon,
her eyes bright as she bangs and splatters
without the slightest concern for moral or even practical order;
the pepper specks on the underlip of a beardless boy too short to
    shave
in a poorly-lighted high-hung mirror whose silver curls lacy black at
    the angles;
the taut skin that suddenly twists when muscles underneath it move
as a Somali beauty speaks her buzzing bee-clouded needs;
the sub-equatorial mountains;
the slack wattles waving good-bye
over the foothills and peaks of apples that belong to neither A. nor E.;
The river that as you grow closer you can see is a canyon,
not silent and still but roaring and pouring toward an unthinkably
    distant ocean
and making music that all goes in one direction,
with firm white arcs like jawbones the root chord.

BOULDERS AND GOATS

In the same floating matter
as light and shadows in the shutters,
as boulders and goats,
as slithering wind and wandering water,

as dog beds, white wine and fever,
think up eternity beyond a forever
you can't in fact imagine, and pass it on; lift
yourselves with images like levers

that turn the weightlessness of numbers.
Then end insentient as lumber,
having lost everything — no, more.

But go on, glimpse guilders in the leaves,
see silver goats and golden boulders.
Never to know is less than you can bear.

READYMADE SITUATION

All numbered outwear will be automatically recycled as
soon as the fecundity of the situation can be addressed.
Participants should address their concerns in a timely
fashion to the fertilizer slash incubator, and that's
regardless of

when the advances, or in some cases actual subsidies, were
made. Legislation is, of course, still pending, but the next
session should bring results, though it's best not to get our
hopes up that the situation will be immediately rectified.
A

more reasonable, or I suppose I should say "middle of the road"
approach is to try to do less with more, at least until the
crisis passes. I know, I know, that's not the means many
of you prefer, but our attitude—and I mean all of us—

has to be "give a little now to get a little later." The wisest
thing meanwhile is to channel energies into productive
and fruitful activities that will ultimately improve things
a little at a time, recognizing that although I spoke earlier
of "fecundity,"

in another sense "paucity" would be an equally applicable
term, though logically, of course, we can't have it both
ways, can we? So let's try to get a grip and do the best
we can under the circumstances. More? No one could
legitimately ask for more.

A Wheeze and a Harkle

Each hunter must pay a fabulous tax before being allowed to mate with a bird of paradise, whose colors are so vivid they seem as precise as words printed with brand-new lead type. Allowed, aloud, it makes no great difference. The chocolate lacks, disappointingly, the residual bitterness of pure cacao, which makes the sugar dissolved in milk both a necessity and an occasion for artistic subtlety. Remember, no matter what you feel, there are people who enjoy your company, even when drinking hot liquid leaves a faintly brownish skin on your square front teeth (who cares about the rear?), and your smile is not spontaneous, which makes the film almost tragic.

So I suppose that means too much sweetness. What do you think? Will it ever all be worthwhile, or must you constantly bite back? How shall, or shallow shall we enter into this, which has no satisfactory name, even though that doesn't mean it's the one god, who is equally ubiquitous and elusive. The colors are tasty as silver nails driven into a coconut, a fibrous existence out of which may be fabricated tough floormats, deceptive Halloween masks, soft cushion stuffing and myriad food and food-related products.

You have to hold that door when we go around corners or it will fling open like a fist abdicating martial responsibility and shamelessly admitting a rigid desire to be touched against the flow of speed and time, for which the dull highway is a manner of speaking. So let the rains begin! We have our seats, and the palm fronds provide adequate protection completely concealing your mother's rage and the milk person's trousers stitched of the strongest dove gray suede, where patent leather (forerunner of naugahyde) might be both more practical and completely harmless to the birds who are ever a twittering fixture of the physical and metaphysical landscape. It's no guarantee of a place for you, only a hunting license. You will have to exercise free will.

SKEEZIX MY LITTLE

Symphony, now there's a concept you can swing from.
Couple 'em up and dive bomb
as frantic as a swarm of wet wasps.

Some sludge is not worth the study
even if in the end, at the close of business day
on Tuesday, you fossick about in the amber

lucidity of the verdigris patina.
Henry couldn't become Lynn
no matter how much she tried to talk him through it

on the phone as she drove to and from work and the mall.
What we call slices of life, a tricky
pond of uncertain depth, of which it might be said,

not wide but not shallow. Let's just say
it's about time. The herder or inheritor, vague
pernicious audience, is always

down in the dumps about something.
Sheep, usually. That's what they all are,
freed from the constraints of whatever

no longer suits you, lateral file or
vibraphone parka lined with calcite
(or seasalt). In bright

moments you feel
you understand and can verify
fate. Other times, the birdhouse overlooks burned grass.

Oh, and How Is the Prince?

And in case you're wondering why one's equilibria no longer interest you, no longer tremble with radiance against the dark stairs not yet stripped and stained Norwegian blond and folded, corrugated but rugless, behind a low door made from three boards, each a dry pine plank the better part of a foot wide, and held together on the inside by a diagonal of narrower and lesser wood willing to serve humbly and most of the time in the dark, it may be because the algal mat gathered on the canal has been sucked up and the water is beginning to move again, not forward of its own accord but with the motion of boats in glossy almost primary colors poled and mule-pulled from a towpath haphazardly bordered with myriad native grasses, or that information may at least in retrospect inform your decision, insofar as it is a decision and not a simple-making response to frantic incomprehension, itself a deflected longing for something seemingly symbolized by dry pie crust leaking hot wet apple slices in a thick liquid of a color not unlike the blond of the stairs to the attic bedroom you no longer have access to, the place you never dreamt of when you slept there and now must long for down the tree-shaded towpath you sometimes see when your mind drops its keys and dives into the dark sea.

MUTTON VACATION

What you feel is always disproportional
to circumstances, which require nothing of
you. The cattleyard was crowded
but I recognize a fertile situation when
I see one, or don't see but only hear
about. The year of the ox they called it,
or maybe it was the ear of the ox,
or the year of the yox. It was not
a restful situation, to say the least.
Even cousin (or uncle) Stephen wasn't snoring,
and he'd been up all night driving in
from some place west where he'd been managing
a Seven Come Eleven which, for some
odd reason sold a lot of Mister Feather:
ten, two and four ("O'clock?" I asked).
The main thing was that everyone was glad
to be there now, but penned a little, wild
in spite of the basic domestic felicity
of the situation east of where Stephen had been.
"I'm surprised this is a tourist attraction,"
Gloria said. Everyone calls her "Glory,"
and I was worry about my tendency to find
(or at least look for) the main thing
while there are so many frantic eyes
to look at, so many desperate bleats.

Stairs/Stares

After I came up the stairs
    the stars were occluded
    deep and shallow deep
    and shallow

You noticed with a certain tenderness

Then there was the time
    you wept with disappointment
    then got the appointment
    glockenspiel
    glocken
            spiel

THE OREGON TRAIL

Detail a subtler prayer to a non-anthropomorphic but infinitely helpful identity, a yearning redolent of slow snow in small dry flakes slowly pushing the huge drooping blue spruce even lower, if inside the sutler's wagon, dry as—I was going to say "bone," but that wouldn't be right, since bone is animate with blood and marrow—dry as a rusty sprocket, a sun-baked plank, a dead root, you could lie on a merino blanket padding the straw-covered floor on the one third not taken up by a path for customers or the counter backed with shelves exactly one foot tall but only as high as the wagon wall, leaving the ecru canvas cover free to shade the dry goods or sun the clientele, could lie on the wagon bed in whatever costume made you feel most free of time, mule boots and a drop-shouldered linsey-woolsey blouse, for example, not ill but only daydreaming, happy as—I was going to say "a lark," but who knows how happy any bird is, their tongues are so small, voices limited to song.

KEEPING ON

With a sure hand
knowing what to withhold
the course of destiny a feel
(field) of density and at
simultaneously the air
identified by light not to be flowing
this flood
                against which each particular
as if in three dimensions
though some surfaces feel
subject to only calculus
accounting for a fourth
                      not counting
less than one hand's fingers lost
to violence (an explosion)
or disease. Fin.
Swim.

LODGED WITH ME

By a four-light window, I'm waiting with a stiffness that aches for and resists posterity, all the time longing for fluency and natural light, even an everyday bulb, bub. Perhaps if I could be faithful, honest, genuine, then oxblood loafers would be my style, and everyone would say, "That's just him, at ease wherever he goes," even sweating in the jungly tropics or having his teeth frozen on the southern tundra of the moon where nothing at all resembles the driest cheese, and all is dust, dust and the peculiar lurid light from tall brown poles soaked in creosote to resist imaginary termites and mild lunar weather. The light is plain and impenetrable as bottle glass.

But enough about light when there's so much gorgonzola here to enjoy and the features of lateral plenty are secure from the marching army of relinquishment, soldiers whose green uniforms are as glorious and on close examination as motley—well, say as subtle—as needles and leaves. Along the dusty road they seem beautiful and specific, less sorrowful and melodramatic than "relinquishment," like a silver turtle in a tin shell held on with the thin sanitary adhesive canners use to attach lids. No, they're no longer soldered.

But what then of the roquefort of the Sea of Tranquility, the *bleu* of the so-called Grand Canal, the veins like map lines clotted in the milky sea, though of course they're veins in just the loosest sense, and cheese resembles lunar nightscapes only if you squinch your eyes and dream a little of a place of blue reflection that responds like a kindly iron mirror to your melancholy beauty, and the light shifts constantly in big planes but never really changes.

There used to be a chasm between December and January, with a steel suspension bridge strung over it. Now there's a pebbled walk. Half a dozen steps will take you across.

And so on, to Infinity

You're both right,
The digits are sequential
And they can be arranged at random.
Furthermore, the house numbers are
  correct, given the order and
  conventions of house numbering.
You're only a certain age for about a
  minute.

Hemp Quoits

1. All Over the Empty Map

To emphasize how important —
Lights hammer a delicious blackness.
Legend reads the map.
Psychometry is a sisterly blurb.
Sketch a detailed map.
We're not home right now.
Please weave, please leave a message.
The machine — a machine churns.
Machines churn and whirl.
Agon fledges a nocturnal map.
A cartilaginous chow handle corresponds to nothing in the terraqueous globe.
She limned her lips.
Her lips were lined, a threshold signal to trigger.
You thought you could read.
You felt you couldn't read.
The subject is folded so it's almost impossible to refold to fit the console.
Which she does, with the veins on the outside where she can consult them.
". . . and every moment seemed on the point of breaking into splinters." (Ishmael NLN)

2. A Politician and an Explorer

Machiavelli and Shackleton had to wear their tuxedos at home because they couldn't go to the concert, for a number or reasons, bowling golden ovals instead.
Now you know it all.

"Of which letigious Famelies here mapped be the Lines." (W. Warner)

All those farm-to-market roads showed the way to the fair, but it was imperative to read along them and ahead to know how to follow.

Otherwise you might as well fly.

We seem to be going in circles.

Maybe we'll bore into the earth.

You won't need a vertical map.

Shouldn't it be on, on the globe?

Eat this glob.

Maps to the stars' houses: five dollars.

Where is north again?

Minute mute scrutiny discovers a way among many.

This template works for all sizes but the tiniest, which tend to get blobby and not at all invisible — no, just hard to read with your head blocking the light.

I'm following you as best I can.

You're the one with the map.

3. When the Rodeo and Elbows

They used to give them away free when the circus was one town over and cars churned the mud at the fairgrounds.

Just give me a chance, will you!

I'll get to it in my own good time.

Are you having a good time?

The trip itself is where the pleasure receives its investiture, especially if you can recover gracefully before you land on your knees.

The spouse was an attorney-at-law.

And tore up the elbows of a white shirt that would otherwise have had a few good miles in it, or outside you (in a lighter vein).

So he takes one look at the x-ray and says it's broken.

What's broken?

The machine.

According to this, your pulse is that of a trained rabbit.

That's why you took the test in the first place, except we don't like to call it a test because you can't fail it, and failure is essential to the idea of a test.

Think of it as an index, a way of finding true southeast in your own considered judgment.

Quack.

The ladder was gold, and so tall you couldn't see the top of it.

The label said, Not intended to hold more than 200 sterling apertures.

And never put a foot above here.

4. Not the Case

I just can't restrain myself any longer.

"Let us leave all boyes games, and go coyte a whyle." (Old Ramblegamp, 1530)

A surveyor's chain of Toledo steel swords drawn from a grey stone the size of your brain.

Insects fly without maps in a leafy, meaty world, wispy whispering wings.

There are no dream maps.

You handed him the map and said, Look at me.

I can't, I'm driving, he said.

The out-takes are masterpieces. Outake in Japanese.

They just need to be arranged properly.

Weight kept shifting until I had to wear a pullover.

Wider roads are marked with Xs and asterisks; *les baricades mistérieuses* behind which the rebels have ensconced themselves are made of hayricks and barn doors capable of deflecting swords.

Whose words?

We are their future and they are ours.

Check the table of equivalents.

How weird to think!

Sometimes I can't remember my desires.

But the books still pile up.

Each leads somewhere.

Turn left at the apple station.

There's a palmetto there.

The trunk looks like latticework, as if the slats would rattle.

That is emphatically not the case.

All the feeling has been stiffened to the point of rigor mortis with words.

"Hitomi" appears on a three by five card and I feel immediate peace, even reading the list in the list of things to have been done, or desired.

5. BLOND STARES AT BORON

I don't know what I'm going to find down there, but if it seems safe I'm going in.

It looks pretty wet.

I'm hoping.

You aren't going in without your hood, are you?

Strike while the iron is purple.

Vast knowledge inhibits.

The streets in that part of the city are bar-coded.

You can't get in there.

Why would you want to anyway?

Two different surveyors agreed on that plat; it can't be seven inches off.

Stood right there and agreed.

If you had to choose between blind drunk and dead drunk, which door would you open and go through?

The way, they say, is always clear.

Cool shadows in the mysterious northeast, the quadrant of dark leaves and rustling breezes wherein the lessons are mitigated by dark abrasions.

Challenge the crisp!

Argue the firm!

Hold fast to the illimitable!

I wish I could be more single-minded if not more specific, this devotion to food processors and jalousies cranked from the street side.

Frontage Road, the longest street outside China.

But it doesn't go anywhere.

If we could diagram the moving arrow and its molecular target, we could understand how little sense

sense sometimes often rarely never makes.

Adroit?

"Yes, ma'am, straight ahead, then through the roundabout that looks like a crossroads there in the blasted patch of ignorance set to music for fear of saying something sententious or judgmental."

It's impossible to be graphic.

Here be dragons gave way to a compass rose and scale of distances.

This ever-expanding landscape.

6. CENTRAL EMPEROR OF GELATO

Another version of a map appears on Highway Sixty-One.

But there are some places you cannot go.

In time you expand with the universe and end up having been everywhere.

Nonetheless there is an end. (The silent speak and stare at mica mirrors.)

It just doesn't happen to be right here.

How else are we to feel about it?

If you follow the plan of what everyone else is wearing, you arrive at the prom in fuchsia, taffeta gown among taffeta gowns.

Why would anyone name a child Fuchsia, it's impossible to spell.

When a book dies before it's born, does its soul go to heaven?

Does it have a soul?

Your very own pillar of salt, one in the kitchen cupboard and one on the breakfast table.

Spell it the way it sounds.

Lightbeat at the edge of emptiness.

Kettle folders, more and more, attorneys-at-law, glib talkers.

We call it a map of the atom's half-life.

For the first half, things seem pretty normal, as if relative youth will last forever.

Then the drought begins, so slowly at first that you don't notice the unaccustomed winds from the northeast.

Weather usually comes from the other direction.

Things seem to start to dry faster, not just nylon underwear but antique tent canvas and wool macintoshes.

Maybe I shouldn't say "start" because you don't ever notice that the elms are leafless until you're well along the road, and when the bus parks under the trees it suddenly strikes you that the shade is mighty thin and the light large, though weaker and grayer than before.

You're already gone, so you can't turn back.

The burnt rubber smell has hints of French coffee, and you take consolation in the knowledge that at least you still have flashes of appetite.

Once you get started down there, you don't need directions.

Just pump along to the point where the magma turns you into steam and molten stone, then wait to make your way to the farthest star.

7. Shall or Shallow Bores On

The Silk Road was long but shouldn't be confused with the Great Wall, which was also a patrol path, and intersected with freedom in several ways. Mongol ponies clattering steps of figurine armies defend the kingdom from men. What else but men? Turn down the sound, I can't hear you. That burnt umber smell is linseed oil. That painting portends a vertical map of a scene dissolving as it was coming into being. Your beauty . . . no, let's take that for granted, or for granite, as the potsherd wrote, desperate not to be confused with the stop-herd. Just knowing it's there gives me a lot of comfort. It's like money in the bank or a pistol under the pillow.

By years of painful effort, you finally came to the mouth of the cave, having crawled from subterranean depths, only to find that the others had already arrived and were enjoying a party to which, at best, they had forgotten to invite you. They called it the Fetish Party, and everyone not dancing was standing around making wry jokes about subjectivity and woodwinds until the first candidate took the podium. You thought her remarks were jejune, but because she used words similar to "liminal" and "carnival," most of the audience nodded approval. Anyway, they nodded.

There was no question about her intelligence or her ability to talk, but you doubted she knew the difference between "ace" and "true value," and would rather read philosophy than fashion magazines. Lavender, you thought, herb of devotion.

Air and fire-retardant, tokens of the ascent and the plunge.

Why not appropriate a bulb of treacle from the clay tree?

Eventually it all comes back to him and her.

Seen in the pale green light of mid-April, the women in the pictures conjured sticks of cinnamon furled like old maps with a U or an S of darkness inside the long curve, but nothing as rich as oyster stuffing.

How do some people veil their gazes when they stare at a lens?

Themes from speech: oysters, raw and moist.

Fetter merchants, let the small birds sing.

Someone has to stay home with the children. It might as well be me.

Multi-viscosity, but how long will the teeth of the microplane continue to shred nutmeg, the symbolic spice of a small nation founded on the usual human principles: separate the men from the boys and give everyone sport-coats. Line the women against an inner wall of the gymnasium. Let the girls dance together.

Marriageable nodality spattering the porcelain tub.

No one uses bluing or set-tubs anymore.

They distinguish themselves with energy rather than knowledge.

No, they know more because they've forgotten less.

Every letter should be an experience: north, south, east, and west, Crow Patrol is the best.

Folded in the glove compartment, the map finds itself too dark to read, but its mood is perky.

8. BLUING, A WHITENER

The open road, the world is full of possibilities.

At some point the numbering ends but the path continues.

All the billboards sing bass.

That bark rocket is also nodular.

Spingo. (Why not Satterthwaite or Shenango?)

In Latifundia the nocturnal juxtapositions are often deadly, but you can't get there without crossing an ocean, which means your road maps are useless as tits on a boar. Take a morocco blimp.

The trails were all laid out by itinerant graphologists whose entire knowledge of the world was questionable, or quintessential.

Still they bred over a hundred species of microcosms that spread nourishment and disease in the salt-friendly enclaves near the pelican coast. I should include Tinea pellionella (in the Linnaean calcification), commonly known as the Casemaking Moth or Avocado Brief.

What they worshiped was a mist into which one day Armada horses galloped, and the world became what it had always been: a breeding ground for sailors.

9. NODULAR

Chart the rolling universe, place of one turn, for you must only turn back when you discover an edge. Sofa and club chair firm on a grid floating in the emptiness that only seems black at night. At the right distance, any small thing can hide the sun, and the sun can't do anything about it. If one of them always wears a tuxedo, the other must always be decked in prison garb. Hanoi pajamas.

Make that, "breeding pool."

Make "a little Mappe or Carde of the worlde" using only ones and zeros.

"As I go rambling around, boys, as I go rumbling aground."

Line the drawers with lavender paper.

You have to draw the line somewhere, but there's no law that says it must be straight.

Holy crustaceans, divine billows, sacred paper napkins.

Musical barricades are easy to break, hard to penetrate.

What's going on in there anyway?

Why are the fa's sequestered? Let them join la and mi.

Who made you the judge and the jury?

Lay about with that sword.

You have no enemies but the indifferent multitude, the indifference of the multitude.

Mulct impromptu dividends across the watery plain where this early in the season green is peeking through the brackish Madaket.

Shall we call it theft if the amounts taken are smaller than garbanzos and are in fact the tastiest morsels ensaladed in the checkerboard bowl and call attention to the inadequacy of the iceberg, which has already begun to go limp in spite of the icy water it's no longer waiting in?

That's why the few peeled things your mother taught you are so important — I mean to say, importunate, showing up on street corners with signs saying "houseless" and looks of devious misery, the subterfuges the truly poor are driven to by impulses so loquacious even a scaffolding of logic and wit can't shut them up.

The shepherd of morality cases pauses, patrolling the perimeter with dogs.

You've got to learn to be more accepting.

You can't always have your elbows up and your forearms positioned to deflect the gentlest lobs of persimmon, as well as the occasional razor flake of flint. Few things we can make will last as long as those stone points. Would you rather cut your own risks? Everyone is so needy, and the peanut butter smells like stale camel smoke.

We really are here, but we don't feel like listening to anyone right now, so don't bother to leave a note under the sisal format. Why, boiled barnacles, young lady! Couldn't you tell? All we need now are air maps and fire maps, says meteorologist Omar Phlogiston, named coincidentally for the blind — well, you know. Crossing the Alps, the army had to resort to killing elephants, which wasn't easy. The whole reason for having them in the first place was their relative invulnerability to arrows and swords, though now and then one went down trumpeting on an enemy spear. Over his bootsoles he was light in his loafers, speared by summer grass among the daffodils along the highway.

How the weather changes. A six star review for the missing pages. As if the British Peter and Jane were much different from the American Dick and Jane, or even the Howling Hyrax. What a diminishment to think of the whole earth as sex, even the geology in its hypothetical layers in and out. "It's all politics." (Rutherford Backscattering)

She habitually misspelled whisper. Sacre bleu! All this and moth names too. I feel the initial tickle of a pin, a mere wisp.

10. Frontage Road

The most vulnerable are the most guarded. Sometimes the bird songs sound as dry as rubber squealing against steel.

Night has never once fallen. All the sparkles suddenly appear as if. To end his map, Hadrian had a wall made. Here endeth Highway 61. Cut that check before the doctor sees it. At the sixth sentence in the progression, featureless magnanimity. Those reveries about Marco Polo were actually a little frightening. How did "act" become an adverb of being? Busily naming things that don't exist: Nova Zembla, Yoknapatawpha, Actuality, the Hundred-Acre Wood, Wonderland, the Abbey of Fillylou over there near the fence where the table feels less nominal and more sororal.

Everyone can be trusted completely to be afraid. Unnatural spring water flows from the rill on the pointed hill. Of course the legend could read music. It was just easier not to. Cookery-books and map-books are the bill-payers, so to speak. So to speak, I said, "Not math books. By no means."

Here we say, "hick, Dick, Doc," because it's quicker and we have things to do, including streamlining the cupboard full of incantations. Arguable everything.

Let's map the progress we've made so far.

One instant equals eternity.

11. Smoked Camel, Silk Road Staple

Well, exactly, people have to eat and go places, whether they want to or not. It's about time. What exactly is the difference between respectful and respectable, and don't just tell me one is an adjective and the other needs to be stiffened with butch wax. One is a bespectacled bald man with a serene votive candle on his head. This is my impersonation of a vizier ordering an afreet back into a Chianti bottle, he said, yanking up his raffia running shorts. It's important to have a firm grip and pronounce all the syllables where appropriate. Root along oblivious of your nervousness.

Your mere presence elevates the moral tone with a metaphysical sweetness reminiscent of cinnamon toast, though of course some prefer injera and tej, or saganaki and diet cola.

Discussion opens pathways for disagreement.

Remember, there's always a right answer to be defended and forgotten no matter how ridiculous the others think you are for defending yourself with such aching poignancy.

Stagger terms. Speak to a neutral third party.

"Diuide the circle at the myddes of your map into 32 partes, pulling out straight lines fro the center to the vttermost bounds of the charte." (1571)

You have a talent you must learn to curb.

One serves on a minor and unimportant committee, but that is after all, one's duty.

Credibility is a key issue.

I daresay always.

Also particularity, so we don't get confused about which stencil fits the template.

Let's float, paddling just stirs the water.

I know it makes you tense to lie on your back, but you need to learn to relax.

Don't make wave lengths.

Just let the water lap.

Balkanization again.

Can you take a phone call without rummaging through your tote bag?

At least you're not being called out to be shot.

It always helps to have something to work with.

We couldn't reinvent the wheel if we argued for a hundred years.

How much difference is there really between the paper you keep and the one you throw away?

What do you mean what do I mean by one?

Just for once I'd like to see a reliable map of the Balkans instead of all this conventional thinking.

Barricades or not, certain geographical rivers are a more or less fluent yet consistent plumber's lifetime. A little bag of doppelgangers.

I have a gift.

I have a gift for you.

I have a free gift for you.

To get your free gift call today!

Headline: "Map sets a path to peace." Sub-head: "Formula could reshape Mideast" [The following should not be voiced: *News and Observer* 5/1/03 1A]

Every time you hit the road you hope it will carry you to peace, not in the grim ultimate sense but merely the absence of the mon(k)ey ladder of conflict, the dappled green pool of metaphysical vision. If I'm allowed to say such things without pulling out the pedometer and strapping it to my palsied ankle. Even then the digits tell only how far you've come, not how far you have to go.

12. Marcelled Hair Made Waves in 1922

I didn't know that was the case or my mind might have been clearer when I numbered the creases and sub-categorized the folds and terrier ears, which is almost the beginning of earth, not materially different from the natural marcel in the trial attorney's back hair, which (to keep your attention focused on the case he had laid out on the table), he would prefer you not be diverted by.

On the other hand there are times when he likes it when your mind wanders.

He just wishes he could tell for certain when the curtains are open or closed, no matter how bright the reflection in the glass.

Calamari and Riesling (just one glass) for lunch leaves the protein diet intact and the yam sprinkled with brown sugar untouched.

Maybe it can be reprocessed into sweet-potato ravioli if we can just step backward in time for a moment, leaving the trailer by the speed limit sign near the shoulder until we can call someone about not one but two exploded re-treads, and have lunch at that vaporous little trattoria in the strip mall while we wait for the wrecker's big jack.

The constant wheezing and harkling of traffic hardly reaches us on the sidewalk from which the white filigree steel chairs have to be dragged every night between the patrons' closing and the real closing when the boss says we can go home.

A third closing closes when she locks up and unlocks her car there in that favored space that's empty right now, through no fault of yours, but not exactly by accident. Hourglass Lake? Cool.

Who has not been relieved to find a parking lot?

A soft shoulder can be a dangerous place to find yourself, though your mind might stop wandering and be focused, along with everything else you're more or less conscious of, on a single object, frantic anticipation, where the tumbleweeds have moods too and she can say no right up to and even over the brim or rim, or whatever it is that's not the place where the pistol hammer knocks the cartridge, leaving a rectangular nock to show it's been used, which you could tell anyway because it's empty but could still be hammered flat and worked along with rows of other spent shells into a handsome brass postal container for the tourist and export trade.

Patriotic paint has the devil of a time sticking to metal like that, though chemistry has improved the odds, along with the fact that gourmet salt is still 79¢ a pound, though you could make it even cheaper if you had a place big enough to dry out a patch, say an acre, of ocean.

Why do you pretend you would come to me if you could?

13. SLEEP MAP

So anyway I was on the train, or maybe it was a plane. Yes, that must've been it, not a train crossing the plain. That's sort of the whole point. This woman comes up the aisle — where else could she go? — and offers me a drink, a free drink, fortification extra, of course. I go, "They used to call ministers sky pilots. Pilots were for boats and ships. Now we have a real sky pilot in the cockpit."

"Do you mean ministers of religion aren't what you call 'real'?" she says and puts a shiny bag of groundnuts on my space-age-material tray.

Half an hour later she comes back and says, "Empty already."

I don't know how many sky miles it was. The air curves up there so the distance has to be measured in minutes, which I prefer to think of as Macomber units, but you still have to circle before you can land and they open the chicken chutes.

Thank you and good-bye is the only way (are the only way?) to salvage a little dignity after almost conquering your fears.

Never, but never, poke your head into that little front room that looks like a cool video game and ask to see the map. Never ask for peanuts either, or they'll know you're not foreign and the chances of the most attractive one falling in love with you will be greatly diminished.

Just some advice for travelers along the black and white road.

Possible side effects may include pigeons, styrofoam balls and mechanical pencils, but may disappear during and after an epicene sensibility.

Please get me down from here! This endless taxi-ing is making me crazy. Try running one of these babies down the Hampton Avenue off-ramp at rush hour in the teeth of a biting gale.

14. Gossamer Doxology

Chart your course and stick to it.

No one in the entire room knew what a petticoat was, or they pretended not to.

Moist patches on the bongo slide again! Oh, man. The conga's already splintered the glockenspiel.

We need a diacritical mark for the inevitable weariness that ensues from waiting on the runway.

A purple smoke tree, I wish I could see it, sit under it, enjoy the shady breezes.

But I'm tempted to return to the scene of yesterday's I wouldn't call it a triumph, but it wasn't, part of it anyway, a crime, though there's not such a fine line between the legal and the moral that you can't step over it.

Leopold was studying Gertie from a respectful distance, and she knew in at least a general way that something might be up, but she felt pretty safe and, in a feeling, enjoyed being admired harmlessly.

Then, without the slightest manipulation, other than what she was doing at a distance and really unaware of particulars, syntax went poof.

Funnily enough there wasn't the rigidity he had previously believed necessary before the astonishing thwarted blurt, and let's be honest about the seventh interval, perishable and durable. The author knew nothing about the actual procedure or he would have provided a towel and a hair dryer. The seaspray can soak your coiffure even when you're sporting a little straw cloche.

A ladder blocking the doorway meant I had no choice but to do the other work, opening the windows to give the room a good airing.

Sorting the pills with a plastic spatula would have to wait.

It all gets done somehow.

That night I dreamt of day trips to Alabama and the freedom of youth with a reliable vehicle. We kept crossing into Missouri in a 1952 DeSoto. The wide Missouri was on the other side.

Tell me again what I am and am not supposed to look for and look at.

Call it a question if you must. Bring me back a Clatsop basket case.

15. No Last Name

Don't think of it as a demand.

I've never won a single award for symmetry, but I go on trying to mold the one-sided banana or the skinless persimmon, with admittedly mixed results.

All right, they're not mixed, just bad.

But the yellow dust in the orange light of the arroyo still suffers fools gladly, doesn't seem to mind at all who squeezes it into her brain for safekeeping.

Mismo is Stephen's favorite Spanish word.

There's nothing like it on the whole coast, the south coast at that.

At the rest-stop restaurant the waitress' bosom was bare and powdered almost as white as her wig, and not a wrinkle under that beauty patch on her cheek.

She was polite and that's all.

Everyone there was accompanied by a spouse.

It was all on the up and up.

The plastic nameplate just under her murex nipple said "Fuchsia" in the most professional tones.

You seem a little blue, I said. Choose the blue door.

You can order, like, a glassy copy of any wire service photo, but it costs, like, thirty dollars.

And there are occasionally obscene pictures of war, or rather pictures of obscene war. Stay the course, in the idiom of an idiot.

It's 8:02, in case that should matter, numbers up in fashionably-colored lights.

For some reason, after we passed it, I couldn't get it out of my mind: sprinklers on an evening lawn terraced with maple shadows and late summer sun. The house was built into the side of the hill, which may or may not at one time have had a name. So there was a one-car garage under the house, and a water heater and pump to the back, which I could see through the open garage door. Nothing, really, but it seemed a glimpse into something tumbling, fertile, permanent.

I went back a year or two later and the house had been completely redone. The garage had mullioned windows letting autumn air out of a wall-papered recreation (or rec.) room. Not the same, but the leaves were still beautiful. I shouldn't say still. They're all gone now, for sure.

Nothing an achiever could be proud of, can be proud of, correcting the days along the salt back ridge of mostly poplars and paper birches with leaves like peculiar continuities, tingling economies without scale, without even the twelve-tone scale, which exists in its perfect form in packing slips and guard rails if it exists anywhere outside, or both outside and inside praxis.

Avocado chrome over gall dust.

16. MAJOLICA, OR MULCT

Your first of what you pray won't be many challenges: using only phonemes, remove the trousers from that bronze statue you're always startled by when you see him walking in the park, and see if you can make him soft.

I know it's been there a thousand months and seems impossible, but it can be done.

We'll watch from the legion of benches.

Meanwhile ladder or lather has been trembling all morning over the creamy parts of the disk.

Let's just leave it at that.

Where will you be when you arrive?

What's that in those majolica unguent jars?

It's make-up for lost time.

It's like there's a conspiracy.

And don't talk to me about baba ghanoush in five hundred years!

As it is now, you can hardly find a buyer for a song about peanut butter.

So let's map out when to say honor bright and when to descend into the giggly labyrinth whose convolutions you've been accumulating since time immemorial, or its practical equivalent in a toby jug of fruit punch and a square-bottomed paper reticule of handmade feature sandwiches. If only we had pictures there'd be no point in continuing, or no need anyway.

The tie rods are bent and the thermostat is all a-twitter, but I think you can limp the rest of the way to Samarkand if you baby it a little and don't run out of gas or, more generally, fuel. The road isn't very well maintained, but at least you have that basket of melmac and those cans of chili-mac in case the Hungarians attack.

You'll need a lattice-work church key and a stainless Amsterdam waffle squeezer or the other team won't jersey up and it will be skins and skins until the scoreboard reminds you of those tie rods. You can buy a packet of shims at any corporate hardware store, if there is such a thing in this era of family-owned shops and carbon magnets.

64

Her high school yearbook sold for three hundred dollars on
E-Bay, and that was just one of potentially a hundred and sixty-
seven copies, most of them heavily encrusted with the wit of sev-
enteen and eighteen-year-olds. If we can just lay our hands on the
rest of them, demand is bound to go up like a rocket.

Yes, "mulct" has a past tense detached from diet and self-help
books at dramatically reduced prices.

You can't expect to do it perfectly the first time unless you're
the first person doing it, and that is of course the only way to find
the meadow or the little house at the edge of the woods whose
canopy offers the most delicious shade, enough really to cast
a warm dappled shadow over the whole future, so that certain
memories get deeper and more permanent, as if the chairs and
light and voices in them were permanent, or emblems of some
permanence that memory's instant replays, insubstantial though
pungent as they are, were verifying glimpses, analogous I sup-
pose to opening a book and finding Swann's curve of jealousy
repeating itself, beautiful, strange, and true in the way that only
detached thoughts can be.

17. "Go coyte a whyle"

But the chairs, the originals, may still exist somewhere, and
even if they've been redone, under the new cushions, the stain and
polyurethane, the chair itself, whichever one you have in mind, is
unchanged and stands a good chance of outlasting the new own-
ers too. Outlast.

That's not to say the reupholstered chair is animate or con-
scious there in the rec room of the new floor plan, by the window
shaded by that magnificent old apple tree too gnarled to give good
fruit, though its golden droppings scent the autumn grass with
sweet perfume.

The perfume ultimately of decay.

In the rodeo of days, Hardesty.

No: Hardesty had nothing to do with "of days" and never rode
a farm animal in his life.

Okay, a ranch animal.

Either way, no.

The numbers were just scrawls so the scanner had trouble reading them, which raised hell with the objectivity of the process.

The map is either right or incomplete.

The gasping season has passed.

18. Utterly Vapid

Everything we know of stillness is informed by movement. Yet I hope I may be forgiven for saying beauty is always particular, in the same sense your Aunt Harriet was particular in her habits, though many find its worship sinister.

Is it more true to understand the layout of the whole fair or to win a blue, stuffed bunny by popping aluminum ducks?

Or looping square pegs with hemp quoits.

Or eating deep-fried extrusions as you stroll the luridly lighted midway.

Die Frau, nach der man sich seht. (The woman they long for.) (Max Brod)

A constantly shifting landscape in which certain objects appear at least temporarily utterly clear.

The utterly is illusory.

Only desire burns clear, utterly clear.

There were all these goofy McGillicuddies, and sometimes they seemed malevolent, but all they wanted was complete control and, intuiting that they couldn't have it, fell back on exercises of will that seemed random but were in fact hardly willed at all.

Busy enough, I say. And busy is as busy does.

She talks about missing fruit but the only fruit she ever eats is bananas with peanut butter sandwiches, and strawberries in season.

Unless you count lemon juice on boiled shrimp and as a handwash to evaporate the smell of fish.

And mandarin oranges in certain salads.

And maybe peaches if she's in the right mood.

And cherries.

And sweet green grapes.

Never mind, I'm completely wrong, though I'd still like to believe some of it at least is a matter of perspective, especially when peaches are out of season, the way some people get their noses out of joint.

Mappy and I are looking at this bronze statue of a handsome native in a fringed loincloth, and she gazes up above the rock where he's standing, one leg ahead of the other and says, "I wish I could touch his thighs."

She didn't mean the statue.

What a thing for a mother to say.

And if your mother wants to die before things get out of hand, and your father doesn't seem to care, who's to say it's worse than shooting an enemy who has three kids of his own and is only holding that rifle because he's convinced your ilk, if not you personally, want to hurt them, or at least keep them from the pleasures you enjoy, or force them toward pleasures they know are wrong. Baby carrots are roots.

We've got to find a way of sharing equally but in such a way that everyone can be greedy.

How unimportant some it is, most of it was, and all of it will be.

19. That's a Lot Like Me

At the mystic village, after we ate and there was a round of anonymous wind-bending, we all bought new sleeping shoes and took a walk by the arsenal of plastic boxes. Nearly everyone found something he or she wanted, and the expense in contrast to the practical value seemed inconsequential in the warmth of the sea breeze, which is how we feel so often, though we're perpetually running out of storage and have to rearrange things and make firm plans about what we're going to give up, Mrs. McGillicuddy. Yet none of it seems as serious as the decadence of the Roman Empire or as desperate as the pleasure-seeking in Berlin between the wars.

Until you face the fact that nothing you do has the slightest permanent value, you'll never be free, and, free, you'll always feel a certain wistful melancholy.

20. Hemp's Cousin Burlap

Dear Burlap, I've feathered my nest enough, though the down is there as much by accident as by design. A nest with only a few dropped feathers can be cozy anyway. It's not a roof over your head, but it helps keep the eggs warm and out of the rain, and I don't mind a little rain dripping through the leaves. If you're small enough and your needs are modest, you can always find shelter and pause in all the rushing around. Where was I when I abandoned you? I'm definitely getting rid of that bathtub full of magazines. Or at least the magazines.

Searching for food for you, that's the wayward plan that seems to be how daily life gets done.

A sandwich and a cup of coffee, or the equivalent in the diet of worms.

People really can't stand peace.

They have to find something to argue about.

The trick is not to take the angles too sharply, bank the turn as it were and try to keep your eyes off the redhead at the aluminum table with a tablecloth dispenser to the right and a doctrinal emission to the left by the padded wheel.

In a wink, a heartbeat, a New York minute, you could see her as Guinevere and/or him as Lancelot, though the forest has been adequately pilfered already, and the idea of dreaming clanky and willowy dreams doesn't square with what we're calling reality in the latest edition of the encyclopedia of whatever.

God put the taco on earth to tempt us, the soft taco and the crunchy, the beef, the chicken and the veggie.

The joy in remuneration and the joy in anticipation are.

We try to process them in the order in which they come in.

You daydreamed of being able to impress your fellow mill-workers with a reference to Vinteuil's Sonata, but if the occasion presented itself for you to speak Proust your courage failed, as if any accent at all mattered in the mound of creosote and degreaser where you haven't worked for years, whether or not you believe you've left.

The building is across the border.

You were often dazzled by what the others knew: the forklift driver who played Bach on the electronic keyboard; the manager who'd read Heisenberg out of a personal interest in infinity; the daydreaming archeologist with a passion for the Maya but on the night shift a robotics mechanic trained on the job.

And you want to sleep faster to hurry to the absolute peace of morning.

21. TING TANG WALLA WALLA BI(N)G BANG

Without the oscillations of desire and fear there would be nothing, precisely that nothing mystics have entered with great joy that can be described only metaphorically as permanent, as if saying "Buy things" could give as much pleasure as contemplating the purchase of a fair copy of Beethoven's Ninth made by his own hand, or the prospect of money to be made from the sale of a T'ang vase in a world where millions guessed on the questionnaire that Alexander the Great was not Iskander Bey but a candy bar with nutrition information printed on its bottom wrapper.

At least a new car offers pleasures you can enter into, vehicle as well as tenor, not a selfish yearning for greatness or connection.

How can a barricade be mysterious when you see them everywhere?

It's not the ones I can see that worry me. (Presbyter John, voyager and emperor, 1276)

Is knowledge the handmaiden of desire or the footservant of fear?

If you want immortality, be wary of brand names, or go ahead and mention them boldly to put them in perspective as rose blossoms or thorns on that bush in the middle distance as you look out from Assisi without having remarked a single bird. Not that they weren't there.

If you could tell when the barricade is down, you'd try harder then, or at least listen more attentively. Afterward I felt so drained and guilty, and not because of my religious education, or not entirely, because the doctrines of that peculiar sect never spoke of the simple lineaments of desire but transmuted longing into a higher form, or at least it seemed higher, so persuasively did it enfold the most troublesome seeds.

No, it wasn't just religion but a cruder awareness, partly fabricated by intuition that dangers as overwhelming as melancholy might come from revealing such needs, such dependence, such willingness to submit to another's desires (not exactly will) and be obligated to pay the price of listening at the wall of verbiage for some sweet note of intimacy harmonized with trust echoing in silence.

Here I am talking about barricades again.

The smell of coffee, which I have loved so much, is stale in my nostrils, almost sickening.

I wish I could send you just the white seeds you need to fill you with what tenderness longs for and intimacy never requites.

22. The Futility of Futility Hints at Meaning

Try Thai.

Why?

It's nice, something to buy.

More thru-streets, neighborhoods, not culs-de-sac.

Accident or design? Is one of the keys, but I can't find the lock it fits, caterpillar key to moth, moth key to caterpillar.

The rules that are written down aren't necessarily the best ones to follow, presuming others have followed them already right to the edge.

The alternative isn't just not to know where you're going.

It's a wonder I get anything done.

Of course, I don't get anything done, but the windows are always, always full.

And the sound of those hammers.

Twelve, an enamel talisman.

23. This Figure Meant

The trouble with you is you're way too serious in spite of the blurts of giddiness and amped-up frivolity.

Open-toed shoes might help.

I think what we tend to think of as god wants us to platform the earnestness, and socialize more to put the whole business in perspective.

Of course it has to do with taste, but you're looking for something more solid, steel-belted tires (not much of a selling point these days of elastic waists) or even good old potatoes in their brown disfigured jackets.

Disfigurement has been much on my mind lately.

You can be thankful your disfigurement has been gradual, though your mind seems suddenly scarred with the stench of burnt meat, which might only be sausages browning in the dishpan, or wherever they brown, all that white and pink.

So that's what a charley horse is.

You kind of wish someone attractive would think, "She sounds like somebody I'd like to know. What an interesting mind!"

But everyone is rushing off in different directions, fragmented sentence after fragmented sentence, while the sun continues to be reliable, as if that might end soon and without warning.

The smell of hair-thickening cream emanating from the woman beside you under the bus is distressing but you can't say if it's the scent or the idea, and you know in your heart you should have more compassion, because the sunshine seems to demand it, holding out the promise of excess until you can't hold any more.

Gargling with salted lime juice sometimes helps, an old trick of the grave diggers' trade.

I was hoping to have a few minutes to play with you before the golfers came back, tartan plus fours blazing like hammocky trees or hummocky turf.

Damn it, here they are, and not far above par at that.

I'm sure we'll hear all about it.

Goober mensch. Even now the cartoons of a hundred years ago seem vulgar, though compared to today . . . .

Imagine how shocked the graybeards must've been then. Wait a minute, you're a graybeard.

And how many times in your life do you get to see a bluebird?

They took the map book with them, but they already know where they're going and what to do when they get there. They just haven't figured it out yet. That's why they need to keep talking.

You're right, communication is good along the metatarsal spillway as on any other semi-vertical fishing program where it helps to be able to map the depths precisely in the still goop and the clear water.

Some like one, some like the other.

They'll probably grab lunch while they're out. I just hope they don't squeeze it too hard.

Once you get the hang of it, it no longer seems easy.

24. WILL

Sleep. Stop what you're doing. Lose yourself in someone else for even a minute. Parts may show up elsewhere. Eat or stop eating, depending on your circumstances. Do anything you feel to your bones is wrong. Try it. I'm talking about national distribution.

We are all: a. traveling breakneck into the past; b. speeding timelessly into the future.

The collapsing map squeals character, whatever that is.

I forget how much I like facts, for example, that ultramarine comes from lapis lazuli mined in Afghanistan, which may no longer be on your map. Or a different kind of fact: that others may remember your sea cucumber story too, even though the blurt of nausea was yours in the sense that you were the subject in spite of also briefly being the object of the attention of the others at the table, at least one of whom was talking the whole time and didn't attend to the stated fact that the tabula rasa was not your sister but a line of contiguous crosses signifying railroad or place of appendectomy stitched up with a curve of steel needle and jet black thread.

You've mentioned hairs already, as in, having the tensile strength of a human fetid nightmare baked silently in a loaf of crusty bread or used as a binding agent in terra cotta — well, mud, really, mud and mud bricks theoretically usable for skyscrapers in Kabul. The sky there needs scraping. Will send planes.

The fifth element, never a smidge of tenderness, only cold will. To resist takes constant pressure, or would, if I could apply it. The will to war.

25. TOPICAL DEPRESSION

Sometimes I forget that daydreaming about God can bring peace, or at least sleep.

There used to be periods of apparent reconciliation and relief. Now there are none. Only yielding the right of way.

The illusion of here and now triggers panic.

Check the map. What's on the other side of the desert? Or are you just slightly nauseated from swinging around those hairpin turns in the mountains?

Perusing a ninth-century *mappae clavicula* from the Vatican bookmobile I understood the simplest way to illuminate manuscripts.

Yes, with swatches of brilliant color.

Most of the population can't read, or prefers not to.

Moving color is the most effective.

A red pick-up truck, for example.

The shimmer of everything.

Mystic easement.

Floss like hair, and golden.

The corpse in the parlor versus the corpse in Baghdad.

Make that Wounded Knee.

The wounded knee at Shiloh?

No, the corpse. Et cetera.

Here and now the heart rate slows, breathing evens out and concentration calms.

Speaking almost any pleasing sounds will help.

"The tente or canopie is made secure by a hempen quoint into which the center powl is thruste." (Prester John, 12: 15 A.D.)

Chai is old hat.

Old hat is old hat.

Would it be well-sucking fan or good sucking fan?

Sometimes late at night I forget everything but this inflamed hard place at the center of my skull, where savage Christians are burning peace at the stake. But it keeps on burning.

26. A Sisterly Blurb

Ramblegamp Satterthwaite signifies personality.

Yet facts are so ephemeral, only abstractions and ideas seem dense and difficult.

Map or no, you keep going. If only you had the presence of mind to glide like the rain.

Would it be too much to say, or the absence?

Never anything unpleasant.

Bad, painful, hurtful, but never unpleasant.

Pineapple ice cream, available in the eighteenth century, and suitable for framing in slats carved to resemble salt and ice though the translucent paint has flaked away, having first faded to white, almost leaves the sentence without a predicate.

Pettifolly lifted her summer dress, and you couldn't resist.

Pretty Polly. Wolly Doodle.

Three kinds of knowledge: weathered, synchronic, and elusive, and on top of that red sneakers, and what for convenience we call sleepless nights, though in fact they're tagged with song phrases repeated in images of boxes hard as oak pallets and hot signs of endless recurrence, though endlessness in other boxes can seem reassuring.

Iron wire, steel wire, uncrushable steel beads like black powder bullets flossed through your wicked convolutions.

Logy. The weave is nothing.

I'm just not going to worry about it.

What makes you think that unhappy thoughts might be more true than these?

As if the borders of personality were impermeable as the identities of individual apples and oranges, the carton is marked introvert, what are you trying to say? Pottery narcotics?

There's something about that pile of pinkish granite chunks that makes me think it might once have been a leach field or could be the castle of memory full of oddly angled rooms in which the most beautiful moods feel as if the images in old movies were not reminders of mortality but evidence of permanence reassuring us that when the details have evaporated the wonderful though sometimes painful feelings will remain and we will leap individually into a new state we will no longer have to keep reminding ourselves is reality.

Don't feel desperate. Go ahead and order that steam shovel you've always wanted.

And what movie is not old soon enough.

27. You Have Time

A soothing little folly like prayer.

Stream of consciousness only flows when you blow into it.

It's as if he wants me here and he doesn't want me here.

I can't understand it, yet it makes perfect sense, what you might call the half-rationality of human behavior.

Once I get through these responsibilities I hope I'll feel more like myself.

As yourself.

Azure self. I like that. I'm a sweet, loving mama and I am blue.

I feel I should mention barbecue at least once, as mysterious as the curl in a hog's tail.

You know you'll feel like a fool in that hat and wear it only in front of the mirror, but it's okay to be foolish if you can afford it.

A wisp of music. The voices in the tower are all the same voice, your voice, I suspect, though you're reluctant to claim ownership of so fleeting a whisper as the slish of sandal leather on worn stone curved like a saddle by hundreds of years of feet.

May one speak of years of feet?

Sand created the gritty sound, and sand is only a raw form of translucence. Let's cook it and spread the bed with sheets of glass, or chip it away until our intercourse is translated into light.

What can be measured depends to some extent upon the scale.

You've eaten quite enough!

A brief narrative of the discovery of Terra Incognita, now, of course, no longer unknown.

Did the gumshoe cover this in the interview deposition?

Gumshoe is a polite way of saying sneaker, just as the opposite of tights is slacks.

This projection is not turning in the way I wanted it to.

At the corners?

No, all over.

How can something turn in all over?

Last night, all in, I turned over. And I think you mean projectile anyway.

For once let's not let our lives be governed by the clock. How about a blind camera?

28. A Yurt

A fully outlined narrative occurred to me while I was doing something else. It was about a person, but I forgot it, a person who did something general enough to intrigue almost anyone but specific enough not to seem annoyingly coy.

Everything I stole I also borrowed.

They could take it back any time they wanted.

I wouldn't be so bold as to say I left it sharper and more well-oiled than I found it, but I wouldn't say I completely ruined it either.

What if I bombarded you with love letters?

Would you recline with me a thousand miles away? Five thousand?

Once I slept with or beside you on the moon in an aluminum tent, a round yurt of a thing invisible in the lunar light.

You were black and white and everything I'd read, lightly made up to accentuate your best features, even if I didn't quite understand it. But who does?

Separated from the blue pool by a sheet of layered glass, we ate sausages and waffles. You put on your glasses to read the menu, took them off so I could see you better. I wanted to swim unsuited in the pool and guide you back to the room but the paper on the floor outside the door said the war was at a crisis. The score was four or more. I felt I had a right to long for Olga, but I knew I had no right to tell you. Footprints create a temporary map. They end here at this sack of names. Before we left you wanted to look at the map one more time. I pined to gawk at the statuary in the pool, but I tried to act cool. I think it would be folly for us to get a collie. They require so much attention, need to pace the perimeter of the property and concentrate the stray sheep every morning, afternoon and evening. More coffee, ma'am?

Salt foam and wet clothes, small clothes in the universal sense, a static clog to the endless heaving waves that become one wave, limitless and terrible as.

Well, shall we leave it, the thing itself rolling and drowning us just out of reach to the figure on the beach, a figure of luminous persuasiveness?

Cross purposes.

4 2 C what E could C upstream with the girls.

The freshness of regret, let's have none of that. It maketh not the smalle fowles for to singe.

You get panicky after awhile but you think you can control it with the sounds of certain vowels and consonants: aum or calm.

The fabric of existence wears thin, wears out, tears, gets filthy from the inside and the out.

We had a nice time at the planetarium. Panjandrum.

It seemed odd to be in the middle of a star-filled night at 11:30 in the morning, like a solar eclipse only longer, but I feel as if I should say "but" and then order foreign food. Sometimes I have a frantic desire to waste my life in measurable amounts. Isn't that precious! We did it! We did great!

And then it was gone.

29. KERATINOUS CHOW

Mumbling his mustache: Lesser lights give more illumination: a sense at once alarming and reassuring of one's

30. DIVINE AVERAGE

incandescent mediocrity.

31. Seasonal Features

The sludge filter is brand new; I just replaced it, but it doesn't seem to be working. The ballasts are buzzing.

A thin fluid trickled through the grating, but there's not a clot of muck in it, at least not yet.

These features are seasonal, like spouses who refuse to move to the town where destiny picked up the phone and said, "Come! Now!"

At least it won't keep calling after you hang up.

The lighter the filigree, the emptier the box, say what you will.

The letterbox collapsed into a blackout of specialized vocabulary known for the peculiar purple of its pickled beets and the excellence of its goatskin fundamentals. When you arrive, a thousand other destinations!

You can go north northsouth as well as south southwest if you want. Ignore the compass and the chart, and row for all you're worth, but try to keep that price on your head.

If it falls, no one will know what you're worth.

32. H.Q.

2. You send me golden ovals in eggplant velour. 1.

4. I send you whispers under the May elms in the gathering dark. 2.

6. I send you isinglass mirrors. 3.

8. I send you a morocco dirigible and the clouds to guide it through. 4.

10. I send you featureless magnanimity. 5.

12. I send you wild swans descending to Hourglass Lake by your asylum window. 6.

14. I send you perishable goods in durable wrappers. 7.

16. I send you photographs of yourself five hundred years from now in a peaceful mountain village. 8.

18. I send you Mr. McGillicuddy; do with him what you will. 9.

20. I send you a spoked wheel made of platinum and padded with kapok. 10.

Key: Parts of this may appear in different form elsewhere. 11.

I send you a painted talisman to conjure rain or sun. 12.

I send you the fifth element. 13.

I send you pottery narcotics. 14.

I send you the paper wealth of nations in sacks of subdivided names. 15.

I send you slippery silver you must not eat.

I send you charming monotony amortized with pink bricks and breakfast room murmurs.

I send you the odors of oranges and anodynes.

In a blue envelope, I send you the ghost of a loving dog.

I send you the exuberance of sleight of hand, the last five minutes of fireworks over the new year, the whole autumn lake with rodents and birds, the feathers of a dinosaur, the ochre imaginings of twenty-thousand-year-old caves, the history of happiness.

As if the intricacies of our minds will save us.

You Send Me

A burp between digitally preserved lines.

Joyce has this to say, "The loose brass quoits of the bedstead jingled."[1]

No one quite believes in another's conscious involutions and involuntary states. One's own condition is always more unbearable and bearable, another's a matter of faulty comparison or weak will.

Some name springs up in the windless cave whose breathable air comes through mysterious nostrils but never creates the slightest stir in the grey mass full of metaphorical caverns, in one of which all of space expands to the farthest stars whose exact placement is impossible for you to know here in the blue willows where the smooth pond seems the center of the universe and no amount of imagining earth as a grain of sand can defile the clouds or make you feel less godlike — as if there were a word for how you feel, alive in the cavern of conscious sensation, where the past has been comprehensively cleaned of a certain kind of anguish because you didn't die then, and the summary gradually became a chart too

---

[1] *Ulysses*, Part 4.

large to unfold, though it was not a Borgesian map as large as the thing it summarized but still only a summary.

I crave one-sided intimacy.

I want to know your secrets but I don't want you to know mine.

We'll work something out.

Misery will drain away from every cranny of the experience it seems to occupy so fully even sunshine can't worm its way in.

The blanched result will seem peculiarly neat and full of good feeling, the way an eggshell is full, no matter how blue and sulfurous the air seems at the moment.

Somehow those are all characteristics of eggs.

Consciousness is hermetically sealed.

Even people with big vocabularies go mad.

Q: Last night, crying in the shower, I tried to get my mother's ghost to come forth and comfort me.

A: Nothing but more weeping, anguish as palpable as a pill but larger, more diffuse, and tending to spread.

Q: I guess oil confines itself to the surface of water; I really don't know.

H: Define "anguish" without metaphor or abstraction.

Q: Everything conspires to tell you you are not, yet you persist in your conviction that the map is neither black nor blank and stands for some thing in some way measurable, a way you must will yourself to go, but which is there all along.

H: There is, of course, the pain that folds back on something you might be.

Q: And joy, so sweet and ephemeral it ought not be pinned against an article.

H: But left to float away.

Q: Between them writhes your conviction.

A: The door slammed in your face convinces you that at least the opener saw enough of you to deny you.

Q: The sugar dissolves, at the same moment sweetest and too tainted to share.

The Way Is Always Clear

Yesterday I killed—Myself —
It was never there — to Feel.
Nothing bleated in the barn —
No one — Heard a squeal –

That's Right, All Day

This empty space shaped like a Cracker Jack™ varnished with Hellenic irony belonged to the would-be hijacker (or hyacinth) who never quite got up the nerve to pull a film out of her tin lozenge box printed in four colors of emulsive ink with a map of the extreme left side of the universe, though the map was unusual enough from a clubman's point of view (a leather globe, don't you know) not to seem a mappamundi in the conventional sense at all but a set of directions shaped like a Bavarian china teapot with a little bitty lid and all over roses and gold and a faint rust-colored stain at the rim of the inside bottom; it wasn't, however, celluloid but aluminum that triggered the tragedy detector, which on certain particular occasions blew its nose and flapped its loose shoesoles in a manner at least mildly comical to everyone but the Irish, whose minds tended to wander on afternoons when traffic was light and that birthmark on your forearm seemed alarmingly unpleasant, as if allegory and irony were as precise as that iron and this alligator sloughing off millions of molecules into the windowed maze you entered by the front door, which was open, and in fact cannot be locked, for you knew all along that metaphor was the answer, though it was a bit of a problem that the question was also a metaphor, and not everyone is capable of comprehending questions asymptotically.

Peony Seed

I keep trying to tell you out of the detachment and spackling will come a transcendence, though it will only be in words put together on a no-longer empty page so that, deranged as you have always been, and in spite of copious recent weeping, you will appear more than sane, more than normal, not only to yourself (easy

enough and impossible) but to people like yourself who will rec-
ognize themselves floating, burnished, in your words.

Marzipan Pachyderm

It's not true that I'm obsessed with peonies, their scents and
symbiosis with ants, Lablacher said, just before her hiatus across
the border through August, month of French vacations and bank
holidays.

She had lost a lot of weight over the years and her joints were
relieved, to say nothing of her muscles.

Her husband Legendre was rooted out there in the wilderness,
a kindly savage in a less than savage place, and had been losing
his teeth one by one.

At that day somewhere on the frontage of the borderless fu-
ture, when the last one popped from its socket, something like
relief might flood through her, for at last and forever he might
guide himself home by the stars.

Periodic Table of the Elephants

One is not one thing.
One is not two things.
One is not three things.
One is innumerable.
Quoits ring stakes, less clangy than steelshoes, less
circumferential than bullseyes.
An eyeshot bull drops.
Plop.
Presumably.
One cannot assert one knows anything with certainty, except
maybe the certainty of sentences and equations, the only things
one knows.
Is a qualifier necessary?
Assert some knowledge without word or gesture.
How often one must act on uncertainty, however violent the
imperatives seem.

Sunlight seems to stream but appears instantly everywhere you can see at once.
Billy flew into a rage that confirmed his powerlessness.
Marzipan pachyderm.
Tiptoe.
The absolute pillow of morning.

TEARS

Caudal uniforms and episiotomies to prevent tearing.
To be clear, say ripping.
The other might rhyme with earring.
This morning, indiscriminate lust, but not without forethought.
Shu-Ching was spreading bacon in a cast iron skillet.
I wept, thought about death and wept some more.
The puzzle of random pieces slowly taking form on the night table is either a map or a wiring diagram threaded with red, like blood vessels. Or just a game for which you have to figure out the rules, an invisible puzzle.

The blood never leaves the road, never steps from the vehicle and gazes at the painted desert or sees the puffy clouds moving slowly as the earth moves almost imperceptibly under them.

The closer dropped a run at the top of the ninth.

The first time I saw the word arcane I was sitting in a black '47 Chevy without rusted rocker panels in spite of the vehicle's age. Mildew mapped the headliner. Crud collaged the floorboards. The quaint foldout: Miss Melanie R. Cane, future harridan and part-time present-time pneumatic float for Shady Lake near the meta-physical doldrums where average white stallions jack-knifed from high springboards and white sheets the size of circus big tops de-scended terrifyingly from the sky. I rubbed that stain until it came off. Cauterize the phonebook and tell the Piltdown Man to get real and stop smelling like eggs. The milk room is immaculate. You can't even smell disinfectant.

Here, these formulas will keep you from hearing anything that will make you uncomfortable. Any time you feel panic rising in you, repeat one that seems appropriate.

You couldn't be more wrong.

That's just not the way I see it.

That's just crazy.

Refrain: That's a lot like me.

Pfeffernüss are not made with nutmeg.

The colonists brought that with them when their cheeks were puffed out like sails full of wind.

There's not much meat on a chipmunk.

Did I ever tell you about the time I slid down the floom into a lake of boiling water that had carrots (baby) and onions (sliced) floating in it, already cooked? They lavished attention on detail because they got paid for the work and they believed in something beyond themselves.

I object to that barbarous "got."

That's amazing! We have too!

It's called money.

Which, since you don't believe in the immortal soul either, means your anchor is without a ship.

That, and of course we don't have a frame of reference either and can't take for granted an interest in anything but you shouldn't say that and food.

And don't forget beer and backaches.

It all comes back to the automobile and everything it stands for.

Freedom seeps in under the garage door and mingles with the oil map on the concrete floor.

My fecund folly.

We appeared in each other's dreams once or twice. That's all.

But he is large.

I blame the medium for distorting these facts.

How often do you see the word numen on the front page?

Your letter made me laugh.

The map you drew on the bottom was a little off, but if you follow it, it should pretty much get you here.

If it doesn't, stop and ask, or give us a call.

We'll leave the machine on.

Tineola bisselliella

What does the map say?

It doesn't say anything. You have to look at it.

Everything was an exposé: Glendenning, the house on Gallowswing Hill, the vineyard, the carriages and carrots (full length), all of it.

Yet we went on, following the faint but firm white line through the fog that almost equated to shame, or manifested itself as shame, not the dry selfishness of martyrdom but a windblown (possibly wind-driven), self-abnegation, so that when he came back from his captivity among the Abenakis he knew more of the dark arts than anyone else in the pillowmakers' guild ever before had. Ever before. Had ever.

I mogul at incitement, the chamois loincloth, the parchment chart in a morocco case, the holy book full of stories that in another context might seem obviously poorly plotted, not as well thought-out from beginning to end as the pastiche of a thousand nights and a night.

You can't just suddenly hop a hundred yards and say, There, I win. Because that isn't the end, there by the geraniums in the test tube inserted into a spiral thingy beside the granite headstone in beloved, in memory, in unspeakable grief because now at last you're complete, no longer a potentially embarrassing loony spattering gibberish between the feet of passers-by on the sidewalk-between-walk, I say, between the shops and the thoroughfare, the paroquet map tied around with buckskin thongs, the blue spruce, the January goose-gray sky: all of it.

Carpet or Tapestry Moth

What means indirection but opacity would want a lock of your hair clean as a spit-washed whistle.

Bring the snip to my lips.

Come, I don't have all day.

You can talk with the others after I'm gone.

Anvil dancing.

No odor of airiness.

Lascars on the prowl.

Omar is of course Homer, blind Homer.
Almond elephant. Webbing moth.
Torch the hummingbird feeder from the nectar outward.
Iridescences return, fluffy beetles.
Put your palm against your cheek and think of me.
You took your glasses off for the picture.
Why?
The better to be seen.
Nothing about your eyes.
Platinum plastic winters now that the.
Your every look pleaded thanks, accepting no correction but longing to shield unsheltered by abstractions now behind you there in the soothing almost opaque sun.

Hammer Dancing

The screw spiral goes both up and down.

Negligence is not aptitude unless reflected in the gleaming titanium screen through which the years, nothing in themselves, pass easily, sometimes one by one and sometimes in horizontal coveys.

Elusive Proustian juices wrung from plump fruit parallel the attar of the holy rose.

Come, and come again.

The night full of lightning and fireflies is nothing to fear, nor is a translucent moon in a blue spring sky.

Cranky or not, the purple-leafed trees make equal amounts of shadow and shade, deftly catching the sun as it turns and turns, rolling on its merry way.

Not blocked by any particular expectation of arrival, why not go on?

Burpless Sea Cuke

What is the strangest food you've ever eaten?
Your favorite basic shape (other than the pillow)?
Do you still ride a bicycle?
Is it black?

Describe your bed.

What do you see outside your favorite window?

Describe the smell of your sheets after you've slept in them for a couple of nights.

Or days.

If you can sleep.

What among the furnishings of your room gives you the most pleasure?

What color are the walls?

Help me think about what you ignore.

What does the light come through?

During the day?

At dark?

What is your favorite foreign gadget? (List up to nine.)

Which parent do you feel you are more like? (Either of yours, or someone else's.)

Tell me a piece of popular music you associate against your will with some experience.

Gossamer doxology, and a faint smell of propane gas.

Do you prefer rose gold or yellow?

PURPLE: MUREX MURASAKI

Edges, limits, spaces filled with things to hear and smell.

Well, not things exactly, and the edges are volatile, evaporating and then crumbling under the pressure of circumstances.

What do you know, Gimmy's got a gun!

What if seventeenth century Delft is more than a blue emblem on a scout's shoulder patch, an image of something like heaven that recurs in simultaneous minds.

Not something exactly, but exactly something in feigned response to this veined emptiness in which Samurai in bamboo armor and conjured whalers gather in pictures against each other like massed regiments facing different colors in a red field without time.

Agon Fledgling Quacks

The circulatory system is a map of everything.

Blood doesn't keep the brain's corridors from being gray.

Consciousness is too sinuous and fragile to bear the weight of the present, never mind eternity.

I wish I could look in a book and find out whether we went to see the fireworks the year I was eight.

I can't remember. I assume.

"Ja, das ist die Liechtensteiner Polka, mein Schatz!

Polka, mein Schatz!

Polka, mein Schatz!"

The talker is always slightly happy but often too busy to notice. The listener is always slightly unhappy, and not busy enough to ignore the unhappiness. They say accumulating money is analogous to constipation, but that's not true. Money is currency. If you have to keep reminding yourself what you want, you may not want it much.

You can force it, for all the good it will do you. What "you" forces? Chinese wallpaper. Dragon flowers. I would hold you close and ease your disease, but you insist on talking, mostly about your disease. Seriousness is a plus. Flowers that never appeared anywhere but on walls. You go through a lightly opened door. On the other side you still can't swim in the air. The man behind you trips over the rubber-backed rug that says, "Coffee." Not "Turkish." Not "Rug." I think a lot of your vulva without picturing it as Chinese wallpaper. The fundamental difference is the way you insist on saying "a" while I gravitate to "the."

It's not that I'm without pride. It's just that I can't think of anything, feel anything to be proud of. My own effort, I mean.

Endless side trips right up to the grave, whether or not you ever go back to New Mexico.

Longing for something impossible from others, from another, has been made interdict by others, by another. Thee.

Still, differences in X are more difficult than differences in Y, and the answer is sometimes a steel I-beam you for some reason can't see.

Inserted from Below

Incorporate the following changes here: Statues mutely mutilated by soldiers of a different religion. The otherness of others. Breadfruit pudding. Good tires. The Buddha incarnated in a stylized image, images that duplicate no one in the living world. Serene pond humming with wings. A ring you fling at a stake plunged into the chocolate earth, the shit earth, the ochre earth, the red dirt. The reanimation of melancholy. To anatomize it you must make sure it's dead. This vast and chilly domain. The manifest ego.

If you get this far call 919-515-4150 for your free gift. (C. Carlton circa 1998)

Inserted from the Side

Perhaps it's coming clear that I don't believe in experience. To me as well as to you. The restaurant where we used to meet. Your bovine but intelligent eyes. All that summed up doesn't amount to. Isn't an experience you can. There's a lack of narrative.

Little whispers are weasels.

A thumped rotted log overgrown with softening moss and lichen. Lie here kin.

Rays streaming through a leafy canopy.

And no big breezes, only the soft thuck of quoit on dowel, broom handle intaglio to the cognoscenti.

Of course the phone rings just as you're.

That perfume is not your usual, slightly spicy, with a cypress top-note.

Sensibility more subtle than despair.

Out of the darkness a dark voice leading you on, the only way is down.

But the earth's a sphere and down is where the orrery never turns.

Only round and round and round in three dimensions, never stopping on a dime, no matter how dim you are.

Underneath the barricade the universe is whirling, and eternity is the turn back at the farthest star.

Cat powder on the folded towel.

What makes me think you'll find any place I could take you interesting enough to go, stay awake, put the pieces together in the backseat until we come to more interesting scenery.

My darkness is bigger than yours, even if you can't see it.

I think I see yours. And then you say it isn't there. What darkness?

I'm standing here in fifty-year-old sunshine light-minutes away, looking at every detail.

Mine deepens or remains the same, only more viscous.

Who can tell?

I keep saying your name over and over in my head. Your name. Yours.

I don't know you. I'll never know you. Lynn, Henry, whatever.

And if I knew you I probably wouldn't like you.

These horses are all dead.

The mules too.

Intaglio Boom

The second day, in the quiet part of the river, we were gathered for recreation. All the girls were in bathing suits except the Asian girl (and she was a girl, barely fledged), who was naked and didn't seem to notice. Or she thought bathing suits were optional, even when men were present, as at least I was. I knew the others would educate her as to our customs soon enough, though they seemed to be taking their time, perhaps because she was so innocent and happy. I was desperate to get closer to her, to see her innocent beauty, to drink it in while I could, though she didn't really know me, and I couldn't be sure she spoke my language. Her wonderful nakedness. My soul. God. What can I do with an image, especially since the soul is mortal, defines mortality?

I hung your raincoat where I still have access to the past.

Let a machine duplicate that.

Come to me, darling. Dreaming of you has made me wicked horny. The carapace inside the dreaming meat. Start jumping the breaks?

Anything and nothing are equally possible.

Painted Polly

Money answers all desires.

Art is dispensable.

Time troubles us.
Time tricks us.
Enter the river slowly.
Repeat as often as you can.
A ribbon of magic water. The keel of the boat's prow. The keel of the boat's prow. The keel of the boat's prow dragged from the cracking ice where it had frozen. The keel of the boat's prow dragged from the cracking ice where it had frozen led to irritated muttering. Irritated muttering. Oh, the puppet fair! Yes, I have not forgotten. The grass has been moved, the cardboard staging assembled from the refrigerator carton, the rain kept at bay. Everything I know says give up. Everything I want says keep going.

Give up what to whom? Often I have mapped the entire territory and painted its head from nearly every angle. (Photos pale and fade.) But when you arrive there, it seems strange, permeated with a beautiful atmosphere you can't begin to put into words, to put into words, to put into words, put words together to recreate (or create), the real life of the mortal inner life, as beautiful and impermanent as sensory existence, which after all has no name — the real wrapped in plastic, which itself remains infinitely fresh.

The matinee over, we stepped from the darkened theater into afternoon sunshine and immediately thought of returning to work, for the soul had flown, and everything on stage had slid into uncertain memory, where nothing should make you angry, gone as it all is, even the coldness of a particular other, who has varied through time but always proven impossible to please, or easier to please than you thought. We didn't know what to say, we were both so afraid of feeling (or seeming, or being) stupid. Prester the Roamer's tuxedo was a tweed tabby jacket spattered with maps of gravy from the canned dinner his mistress (owner?) had served him that night — last night, or so it seemed. It's not that I can't sleep. I'm afraid of waking up.

THE ABSOLUTE PEACE OF MORNING

Golden soldiers asleep under the Iliad tree, between battles.
Eternity is in the interstices,
without which the weave would be nothing.

About the Author

Thomas David Lisk is a professor of English at North Carolina State University, where he teaches literature and occasionally journalism. His previous publications include a poetry collection, *Aroma Terrapin*, and a chapbook, *A Short History of Pens Since the French Revolution*, as well as poems, short fiction and essays in many literary magazines and newspapers.

Free Verse Editions

Edited by Jon Thompson

2006

Physis by Nicolas Pesque, translated by Cole Swensen
Puppet Wardrobe by Daniel Tiffany
These Beautiful Limits by Thomas Lisk
The Wash by Adam Clay

2005

A Map of Faring by Peter Riley
Signs Following by Ger Killeen
Winter Journey [*Viaggio d'inverno*] by Attilio Bertolucci, translated by Nicholas Benson

www.ingramcontent.com/pod-product-compliance
Lightning Source LLC
Chambersburg PA
CBHW032022090426
42741CB00006B/698

9 781932 559965